D0520982

MYNOT PHONTY'S
BONGOSOK

HarperPerennial
A Division of HarperCollinsPublishers

Designed by Gary Marsh / Gone Loco, London
Illustrated by Terry Gilliam, Gary Marsh, John Hurst
Music edited by John Du Prez

How to Play the Piano

1. **Select the right key**

2. **Put it in the piano and open it**

(not essential, if you can't play)

3. **Once the piano is fully open, put your fingers on top of the notes**

4. **Move your fingers about, making sure they hit the right notes**

in the correct order*

5. **Watch your friends be amazed**

* Like a pianist

For other instruments:
The same thing but without the piano

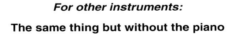

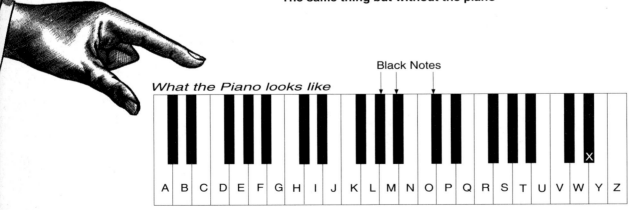

What the Piano looks like

Black Notes

A B C D E F G H I J K L M N O P Q R S T U V W Y Z

Coming soon - How to read music

the fairly

incomplete

& rather badly illustrated

Monty Python

song book

Foreword by Elvis Presley
Middleword by God
Afterword by Brigadier N.Q.T.F.Sixpence

A Foreword by Elvis Presley

Hi. You know, whenever I'm browsing through a shopping mall, or busy buying groceries at a supermarket, I often find myself humming one of the many happy songs that these Monty Python guys have churned out over the years.

"I'm a lumberjack and I'm okay," I'll find myself crooning as I tip a grocery clerk a new pink Cadillac, or "Isn't it awfully nice to have a penis," I'll sing as I buy some more Listerine.

It's amazing how often I find myself breaking into "Ya Di Bucketty", especially when the holidays come around. How I wish I could have that on my Christmas album. And I'd give anything to have recorded the "Bruces' Philosophers Song", instead of "All Shook Up".

Listen, if you ask me these guys are the greatest, and if only I were alive today I would be covering some of their epoch-making songs. But excuse me now y'all, as I have to go out and visit some more supermarkets, so the folks in America will know I'm still around.

Hope ya enjoy this book as much as me,

Elvis Aaron Presley

HOW TO READ THE MUSIC IN THIS BOOK.

Some of the notes in this book are very old indeed. Mozart is known to have used several of them and Beethoven too was not averse to putting them in his songs.

The Pythons have selected the best of these notes to be in their songbook.

Note **E** looks like this:

Note **F** " "

Note **G** " "

Note **A** " "

Note **B** " "

Note **C** " "

Note **D** " "

Note **E** (again) "

Note **H** (not recommended)

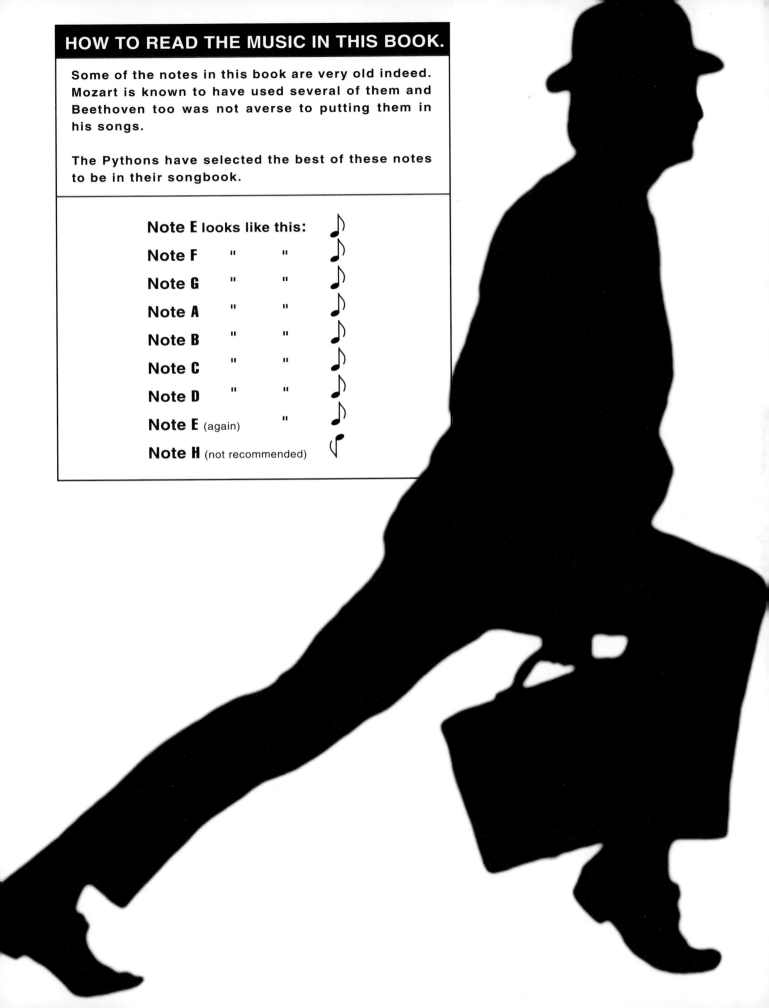

WONDERFUL

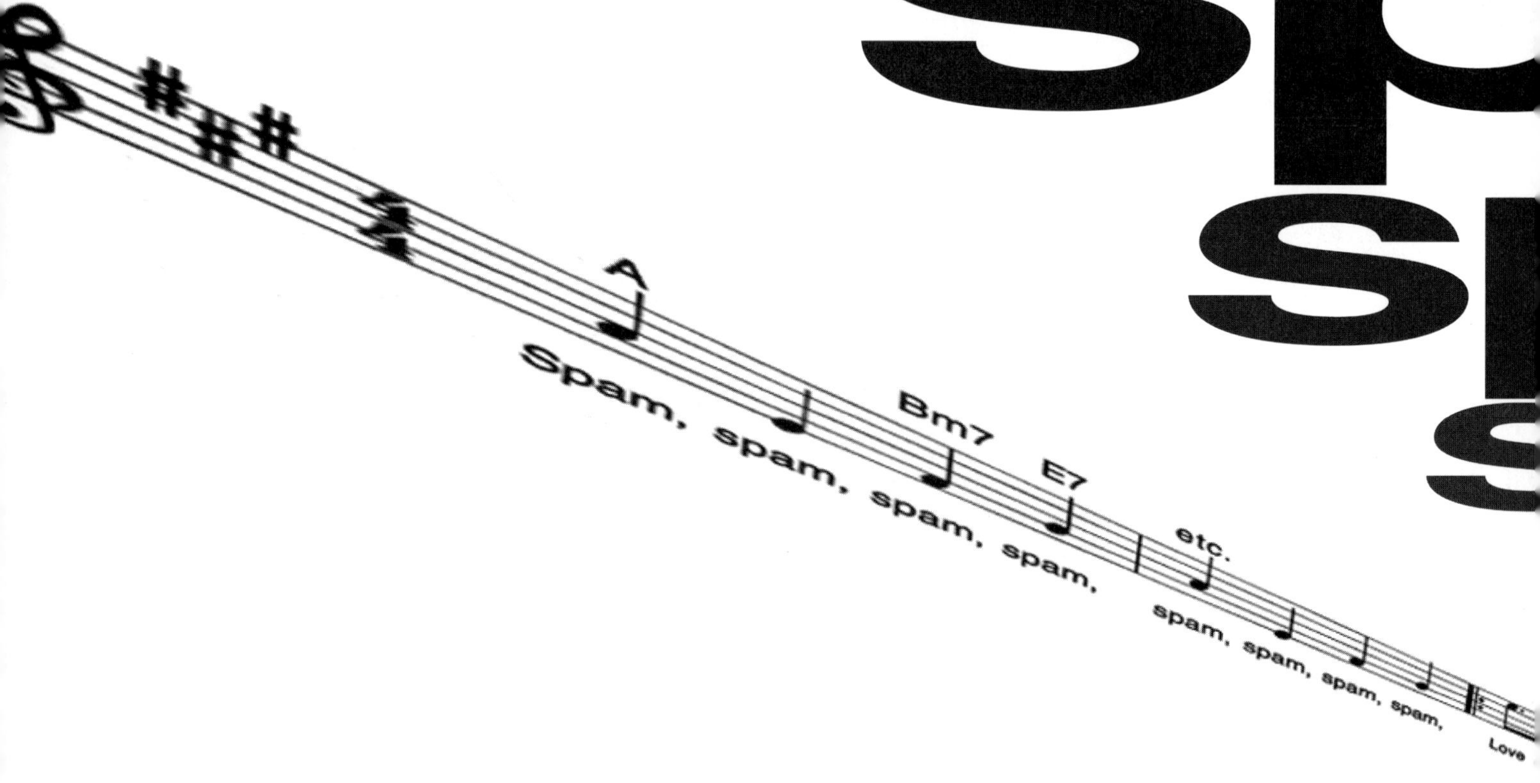

Spam, spam, spam, spam,

Bm7   E7   etc.

spam, spam, spam, spam,

Love

am
am
pam
pam
spam

LOVELY

spam
spam
spam
spam
spam
spam
spam

SP-A-A-A-A-A-AM
Greasy Spoon
<u>Menu</u>

Egg and bacon

Egg, sausage and bacon

Egg and spam

Egg, bacon and spam

Egg, bacon, sausage and spam

Spam, bacon, sausage and spam

Spam, egg, spam, spam, bacon and spam

Spam, spam, spam, egg and spam

Spam, spam, spam, spam, spam, spam, baked beans, spam, spam, spam and spam

or

Lobster thermidor aux crevettes with mornay sauce garnished with truffle pate, brandy and fried egg on top and spam

137

O LORD PLEASE DON'T BURN US

Traditional Irish Melody
Harmony by Erik Constrictor 1166-72

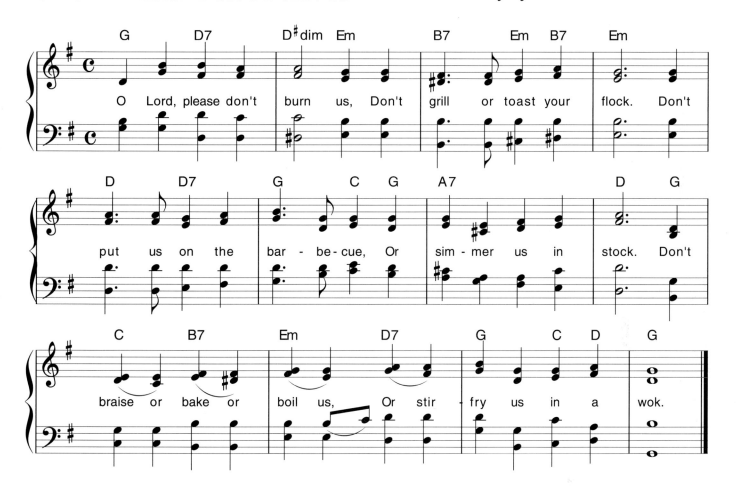

O LORD, please don't burn us,
Don't grill or toast your flock,
Don't put us on the barbecue,
Or simmer us in stock,
Don't braise or bake or boil us,
Or stir-fry us in a wok.

2* Oh please don't lightly poach us,
Or baste us with hot fat,
Don't fricassee or roast us,
Or boil us in a vat,
And please don't stick thy servants, Lord,
In a Rotissomat.

Latin, VENANTIUS FORTUNATUS 530-609
Tr W. CHATTERTON DIX 1837-98
and others

*For descant version, see over

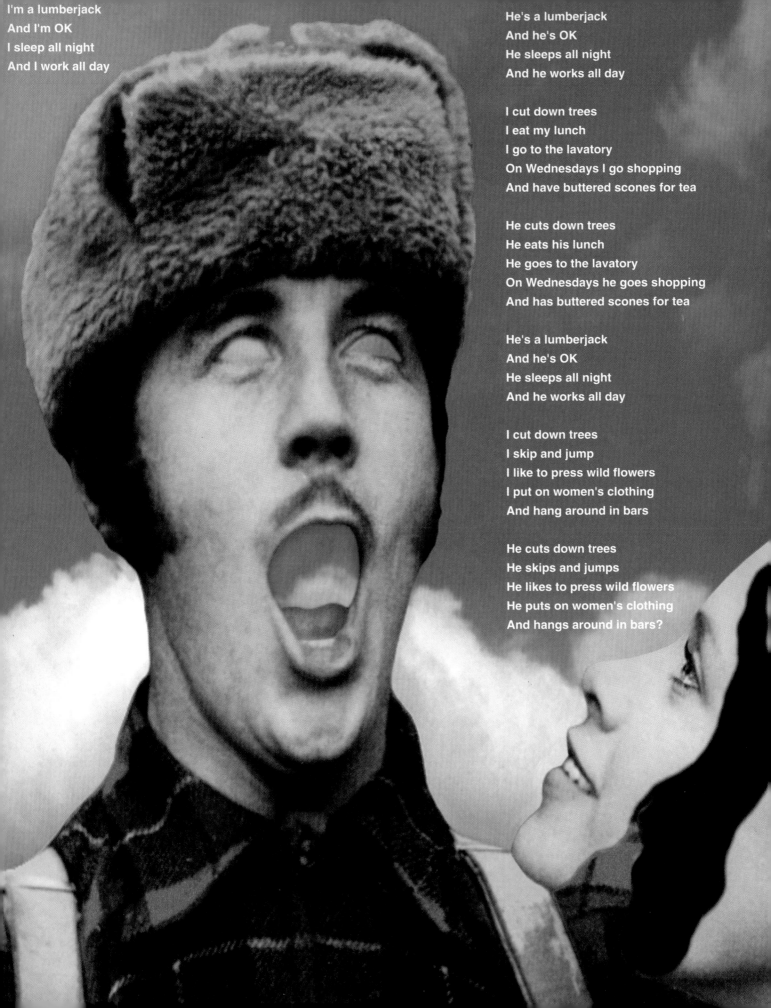

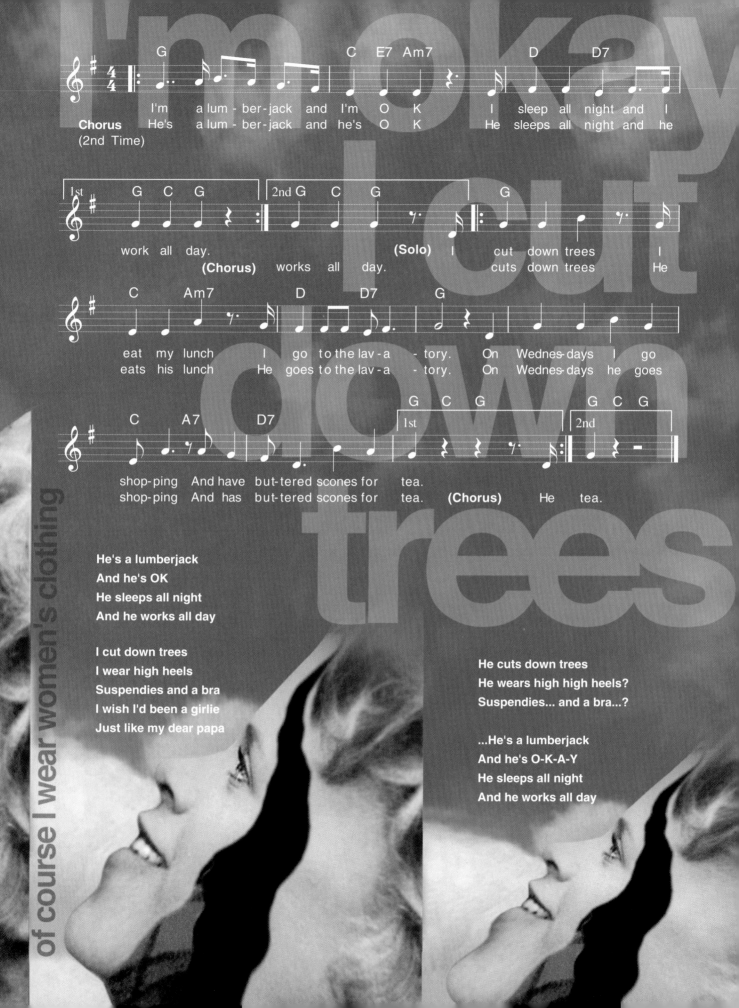

Ich bin ein Holzfäller und fühl mich stark
Ich schlaf des Nachts und hack am Tag

Er ist ein Holzfäller und fühlt sich stark
Er schläft des Nachts und hackt am Tag

Ich fälle Bäume, ich ess mein Brot
Ich geh auf das WC
Am Mittwoch geh ich shopping
Kau Kekse zum Kaffee

Er fällt die Bäume er isst sein Brot
Er geht auf das WC
Am Mittwoch geht er shopping
Kaut Kekse zum Kaffee

Er ist ein Holzfäller und fühlt sich stark
Er schläft des Nachts und hackt am Tag

Ich fälle Bäume und hupf und spring
Steck Blumen in die Vas
Ich schlupf in Frauenkleider
Und hummel mich in Bars

Er fällt Bäume, er hupft und springt
Steckt Blumen in die Vas
Er schlupft in Frauenkleider
Und hummelt sich in Bars...?

Er ist ein Holzfäller und fühlt sich stark
Er schläft des Nachts und hackt am Tag

Ich fälle Bäume, trag Stöckelschuh
Und Strumpf und Bustenhalter
Wär gern ein kleines Mädchen
So wie mein Onkel Walter

Er fällt die Bäume, trägt Stöckelschuh
Und Strumpf und Bustenhalter...?

Mister

Dennis Moore

Dennis Moore, Dennis Moore
Galloping through the sward
Dennis Moore, Dennis Moore
And his horse Concorde
He steals from the rich
And gives to the poor
Mr Moore, Mr Moore, Mr Moore

Dennis Moore, Dennis Moore
Riding through the night
Soon every lupin in the land
Will be in his mighty hand
He steals them from the rich
And gives them to the poor
Mr Moore, Mr Moore, Mr Moore

Dennis Moore, Dennis Moore
Dum dum dum the night
Dennis Moore, Dennis Moore
Dum de dum dum plight
He steals dum dum dum
And dum dum dum dee
Dennis dum, Dennis dee, dum dum dum

Dennis Moore, Dennis Moore
Riding through the woods
Dennis Moore, Dennis Moore
With a bag of things
He gives to the poor
And he takes from the rich
Dennis Moore, Dennis Moore, Dennis Moore

Dennis Moore, Dennis Moore
Riding through the land
Dennis Moore, Dennis Moore
Without a merry band
He steals from the poor
And gives to the rich
Stupid bitch

I can see a bare-bottomed mandrill

Slyly eyeing his upper nostril

If he jumps inside there too

I really won't know what to do

I'll be a proud possessor of a kind of nasal zoo

A nasal zoo

I've got a ferret sticking up my nose

And what is worse it constantly explodes

Ferrets don't explode you say

But it happened nine times yesterday

And I should know 'cause each time

I was standing in the way

I've got a ferret sticking up my nose

I've got a ferret sticking up my nose

How it got there I can't tell

But now it's there it hurts like hell

And what is more it radically affects

my sense of smell

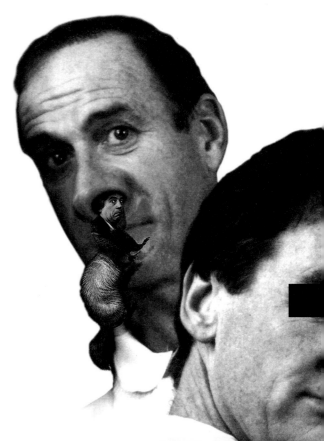

ferret song

I've got a fer - ret stick - ing up my nose. **(Chorus)**

He's got a fer - ret stick - ing up his nose. **(Solo)** How it got there

I can't tell But now it's there it hurts like hell And what is more it

rad - i - cally af - fects my sense of smell. (His sense of smell.)

There is nothing quite as wonderful as money
There is nothing like a newly minted pound
Everyone must hanker
For the butchness of a banker
It's accountancy that makes the world go round

You can keep your Marxist ways
For it's only just a phase
For it's money makes the world go round

Bruces'

Philosophers Song

Immanuel Kant was a real piss ant
Who was very rarely stable,
Heidegger, Heidegger was a boozy beggar
Who could think you under the table,
David Hume could out-consume
Wilhelm Friedrich Hegel,
And **Wittgenstein** was a beery swine
Who was just as schloshed as **Schlegel**.
There's nothing **Nietzsche** couldn't teach ya
'Bout the raising of the wrist,
Socrates, himself, was permanently pissed.

John Stuart Mill, of his own free will,
On half a pint of shandy was particularly ill,
Plato, they say, could stick it away,
Half a crate of whisky every day.
Aristotle, Aristotle was a bugger for the bottle,
Hobbes was fond of his dram,
And **René Descartes** was a drunken fart,
"I drink, therefore I am."
Yes **Socrates**, himself, is particularly missed,
A lovely little thinker,
But a bugger when he's pissed.

MUDDY KNEES

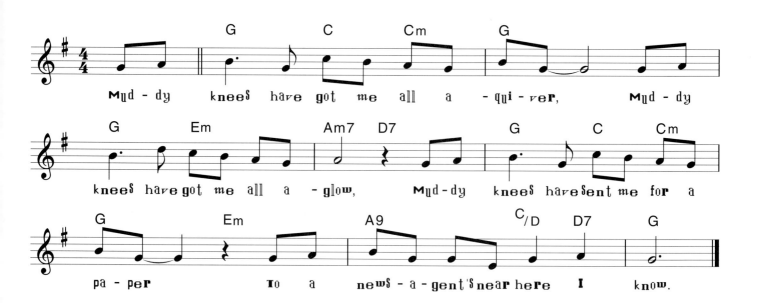

Mud-dy knees have got me all a-qui-ver, Mud-dy knees have got me all a-glow, Mud-dy knees have sent me for a pa-per To a news-a-gent's near here I know.

Fa la la la la la la la la la la la la la la la la la la la la la la la la la la la la la la

SUMMARIZING PROUST

GONGgggg !

Brave Sir Robin.

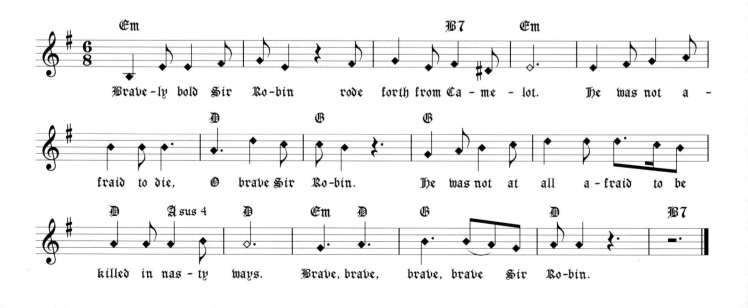

Brave-ly bold Sir Ro-bin rode forth from Ca-me-lot. He was not a-
fraid to die, O brave Sir Ro-bin. He was not at all a-fraid to be
killed in nas-ty ways. Brave, brave, brave, brave Sir Ro-bin.

Bravely bold Sir Robin rode forth from Camelot

He was not afraid to die, o brave Sir Robin

He was not at all afraid to be killed in nasty ways

Brave, brave, brave, brave Sir Robin

He was not in the least bit scared to be mashed into a pulp

Or to have his eyes gouged out and his elbows broken

To have his kneecaps split and his body burned away

And his limbs all hacked and mangled, brave Sir Robin

His head smashed in and his heart cut out

And his liver removed and his bowels unplugged

And his nostrils raped and his bottom burnt off and his penis...

He is brave Sir Robin,

Brave Sir Robin who...

To fight and.............

Brave Sir Robin ran away

Bravely, ran away... away...

When danger reared its ugly head

He bravely turned his tail and fled

Yes, brave Sir Robin turned about

And gallantly he chickened out

Bravely taking to his feet

He beat a very brave retreat

Bravest of the brave, Sir Robin

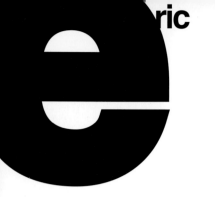

A-one,
two, a-one
two three four

Half a bee, philosophically,
must *ipso facto* half not be.
But half the bee, has got to be,
vis-a-vis its entity. D'you see? But can
a bee be said to be, or not to be an entire bee,
when half the bee is not a bee, due to some ancient injury?

La di di, one two three, Eric the half a bee. A B C D E F G, Eric the half a bee.

Is this wretched demi-bee, half asleep upon my knee, some freak from a menagerie? No!
It's Eric the half a bee. Fiddle di dum, fiddle di dee, Eric the half a bee. Ho ho ho, tee hee hee,
Eric the half a bee.

I love this hive employ-ee-ee, bisected accidentally, one summer afternoon by me, I love him carnally.
He loves him carnally...Semi-carnally. The end. Cyril Connolly?
No, semi-carnally.   Oh.

Cyril Connolly   (Ends with elaborate whistle)

Yum yu

Rum

C   C

(Yum yum) Yum   yum   di   buc - ket - ty,   Rum   ting   phu-taow,
          (All)   Ya   di   buc - ket - ty,   Rum   ting   phu-taow,

Dm   C

Yi   ni   ni,   Yaowww!
Yi   ni   ni,   Yaowww!

Mmm, that's a good idea for a song, mmh...on second thoughts go down

Yum yum di buckett /

Yum yum di

Yum yum di bucketty

Rum ting phutaow

Yi Ni Ni

Yaowww!

Rum ting

Rum ting phutaow

Yi Ni Ni

Ya di bucketty

Rum ting phutaow

Yi Ni Ni

Yaowww!

Yaowww!

ad and get me twenty Rothmans

Yaowwww!

Rhubarb Tart . . .

I want another slice of rhubarb tart
I want another lovely slice
I'm not disparaging the blueberry pie
But rhubarb tart is oh-so-very nice

A rhubarb what? A rhubarb tart
A what-barb tart? A *rhu*-barb tart
I want another slice of rhubarb tart

The principles of modern philosophy
Were postulated by Descartes
Discarding everything he wasn't certain of
He said, "I think therefore I am a rhubarb tart"

A rhubarb what? A rhubarb tart
René who? René Descartes
Poor mutt, he thought he was a rhubarb tart

Rhubarb tart has fascinated all the poets
Especially the Immortal Bard
He made Richard the Third call out at Bosworth Field
"My kingdom for a slice of rhubarb tart"

Immortal what? Immortal tart
Rhubarb what? A rhubarb Bard
As rhymes go that is really pretty bad

I want a-no-ther slice of rhu-barb tart. I want a-no-ther
love-ly slice. I'm not dis-pa-ra-ging the blue-berry pie, But
rhu-barb tart is oh so ve-ry nice.

Chorus

a rhu-barb tart.
A rhu-barb what? A what-barb
a rhu-barb tart. I want a-no-ther slice of rhu-barb tart.
tart? I want a-no-ther slice of rhu-barb tart.

Since Wassily Kandinsky and Paul Klee
Laid down the axioms of abstract art
Even Jackson Pollock and Piet Mondrian
Prefer to paint a slice of rhubarb tart

Wassi who? A Wassi-ly
Kandin who? A Kandin-sky
And how did he get in there for a start?

Read all the existentialist philosophers
Like Schopenhauer and Jean-Paul Sartre
Even Martin Heidegger agreed on one thing
Eternal happiness is rhubarb tart

A rhubarb what? A rhubarb tart
Jean-Paul who? Jean-Paul Sartre
That sounds just like a rhyme from Lionel Bartre

I want another slice of rhubarb tart
I want another lovely slice
I'm not disparaging the blueberry pie
But rhubarb tart is oh-so-very nice

bang

Bing tiddle tiddle

Bung tiddle tiddle bang

Bung tiddle tiddle tiddle tiddle tiddle

Bung tiddle tiddle **bong**

Bung tiddle tiddle bing

Bung tiddle tiddle bang

Bing tiddle tiddle

Bang tiddle tiddle

Bong tiddle tiddle

Bing tiddley ding **ding** bang bong

A Song for Europe

How they fared:

1st: Monaco with "Bing Tiddle Tiddle Bong"
2nd: Italy with "Si Si Boing Bang"
3rd: Germany with "Nein Bong Über Tiddle"
Equal 4th: England with "Bang Bang Bang Bang"
          Ireland with "Ay Ay Ay Ay"
          Scotland with "Och Och Och Och"
          Israel with "Oy Oy Oy Oy"
5th: France with "Post Coitum Omnia Animal Tristes Est"
6th: Sweden with "Ding Ding A Dong"

Yangtse Song

We love the Yangtse, Yangtse Kiang
Flowing from Yushu down to Ching Kiang
Passing through Chung King, Wuhan and Hoo Kow
Three thousand miles, but it gets there somehow

Oh! Szechuan's the province and Shanghai is the port
And Yangtse is the river that we all support

We love the Yang-tse Yang-tse-Ki-ang Flo-wing from Yu-shu
Down to Ching-Ki-ang Pas-sing through Chung-King, Wu-han and Hoo-Kow
Three thou-sand miles But it gets there some-how Oh! Sze-chuan's the pro-vince And
Shang-hai is the port, And Yang-tse's the ri-ver that we all sup-port.

Oliver Cromwell

(Chopin Polonaise No. 6 Op. 53 in A flat)

The most interesting thing about King Charles I is that he was 5'6" tall at the start of his reign,
but only 4'8" tall at the end of it... because of...

But under the terms of John Pimm's solemn league and covenant, the Scots handed King Charles I over to...

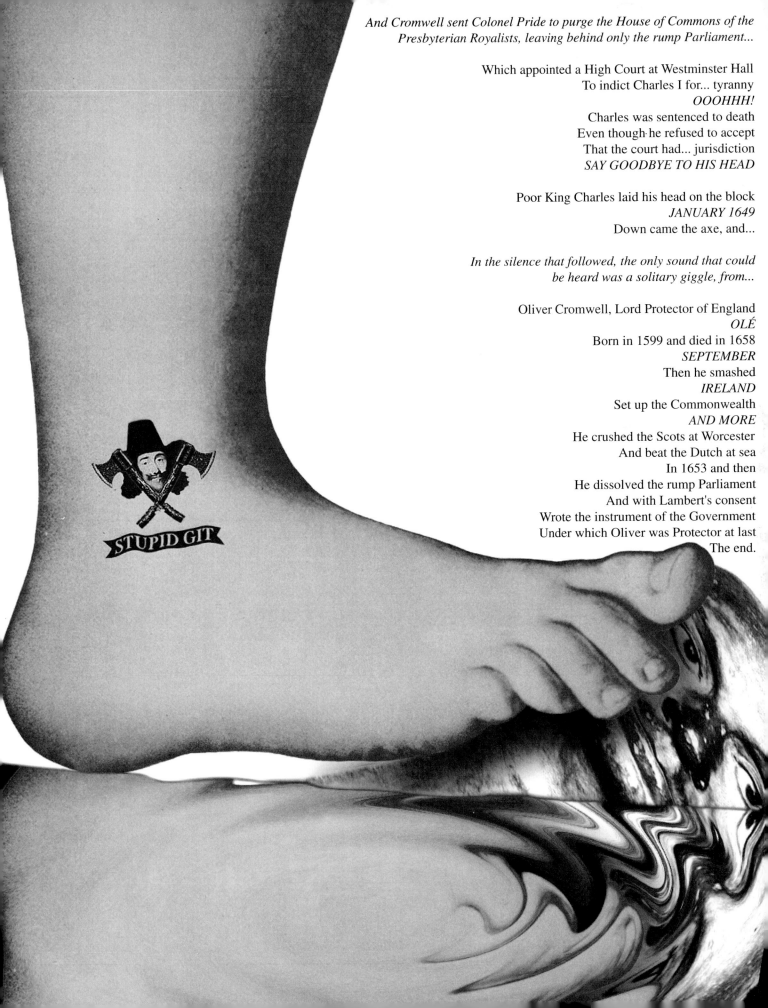

And Cromwell sent Colonel Pride to purge the House of Commons of the Presbyterian Royalists, leaving behind only the rump Parliament...

Which appointed a High Court at Westminster Hall
To indict Charles I for... tyranny
OOOHHH!
Charles was sentenced to death
Even though he refused to accept
That the court had... jurisdiction
SAY GOODBYE TO HIS HEAD

Poor King Charles laid his head on the block
JANUARY 1649
Down came the axe, and...

*In the silence that followed, the only sound that could
be heard was a solitary giggle, from...*

Oliver Cromwell, Lord Protector of England
OLÉ
Born in 1599 and died in 1658
SEPTEMBER
Then he smashed
IRELAND
Set up the Commonwealth
AND MORE
He crushed the Scots at Worcester
And beat the Dutch at sea
In 1653 and then
He dissolved the rump Parliament
And with Lambert's consent
Wrote the instrument of the Government
Under which Oliver was Protector at last
The end.

STUPID GIT

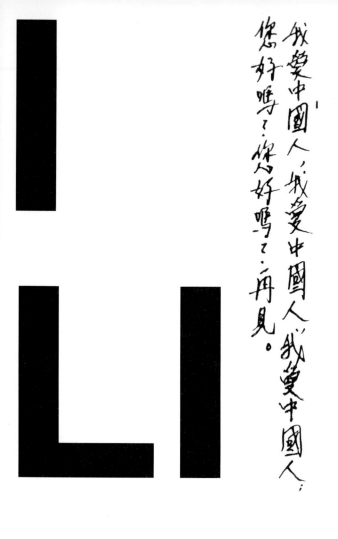

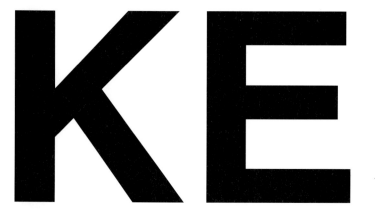

I
LI
KE

我愛中國人，我愛中國人，我愛中國人；您好嗎？您好嗎？再見。

The world today seems absolutely crackers
With nuclear bombs to blow us all sky high
There's fools and idiots sitting on the trigger
It's depressing and it's senseless and that's why...

I like Chinese
I like Chinese
They only come up to your knees
Yet they're always friendly
And they're ready to please

I like Chinese
I like Chinese
There's nine hundred million of them
In the world today
You'd better learn to like them
That's what I say

I like Chinese
I like Chinese
They come from a long way overseas
But they're cute and they're cuddly
And they're ready to please

I like Chinese food
The waiters never are rude
Think of the many things they've done to impress
There's Maoism, Taoism, I Ching and chess

So I like Chinese
I like Chinese
I like their tiny little trees
Their Zen, their ping-pong, their yin and yang-ese

I like Chinese thought
The wisdom that Confucius taught
If Darwin is anything to shout about
The Chinese will survive us all without any doubt

So I like Chinese
I like Chinese
They only come up to your knees
Yet they're wise and they're witty
And they're ready to please

I like Chinese
I like Chinese
Their food is guaranteed to please
A fourteen, a seven, a nine and lychees

I like Chinese
I like Chinese
I like their tiny little trees
Their Zen, their ping-pong, their yin and yang-ese

I like Chinese...

Knights of the Round Table

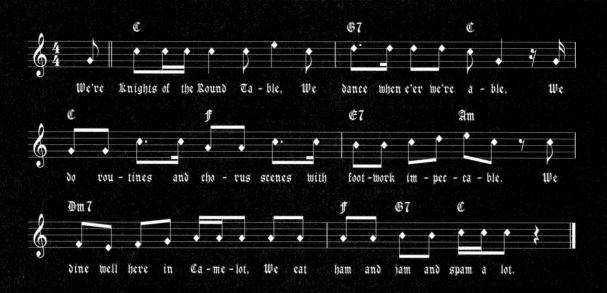

We're Knights of the Round Table,
We dance when e'er we're able,
We do routines and chorus scenes
    with footwork impeccable.

We dine well here in Camelot,
We eat ham and jam and Spam a lot.

We're Knights of the Round Table,
Our shows are formidable,
But many times, we're given rhymes
    that are quite unsingable.

We're opera-mad in Camelot,
We sing from the diaphragm a l...o...o...o...t.

In war we're tough and able,
Quite indefatigable,
Between our quests, we sequin vests
    and impersonate Clark Gable.

It's a busy life in Camelot,
I have to push the pram a lot.

MUSICAL QUIZ
ON THIS PAGE ARE HIDDEN 16 FAMOUS TESTICLES. CAN YOU FIND THEM?

Other uses of the number 1

1. There's one!

2. In conjunction with 2 to make 12

3. At the grocer's: "1 teabag please."

4. In the kitchen: I (please note this is NOT a use of 1 but the capital first person singular) *have brought my grandmother 1 of these...*

and many more.

Here comes an

Here it come

Here com

When w

ther one

again

another one

it ever end ?

I know whatever it is
I've not seen one before
But here comes another one
And here comes a bunch of 'em
Here comes another one
Thank God I'm not having lunch with them

F

Here comes a - no-ther one,   Here it comes a - gain

C7   F

Here comes a - no-ther one,   When will it e - ver end?

HENRY KISSINGER

G
Hen-ry Kis-sing-er

D+5
How I'm mis-sing yer

G
You're the Doc-tor

G7
of my dreams

C7
With your crink-ly hair   and your glas-sy stare

G
And your ma-chia-vel - lian schemes

A7
I know they say that

you are ve-ry vain

D
And short and fat and pu-shy   but at

D7
least you're not in - sane

D+5

G
Hen-ry Kis-sing-er

How I'm

A7
mis-sing yer

D7
And wish-ing you were

G
here.

Henry Kissinger
How I'm missing yer
You're so chubby and so neat
With your funny clothes and your squishy nose
You're like a German parakeet
All right so people say that you don't care
But you've got nicer legs than Hitler
And bigger tits than Cher
Henry Kissinger
How I'm missing yer
And wishing you were here

The Background to History

(from the hit Broadway musical *An Introduction to the Open Field System in Mediaeval England Part IV*)

A new series on Radio 3, introduced by Professor Angus Jones of the Open University
Part IV: The Open Field Farming System in Mediaeval England

PROF. JONES: One of the main elements in any study of the mediaeval open-field
farming system is the allocation of plough teams for the winter sowing.
Professor Tofts of the University of Manchester puts it like this:

Molto Marlioso

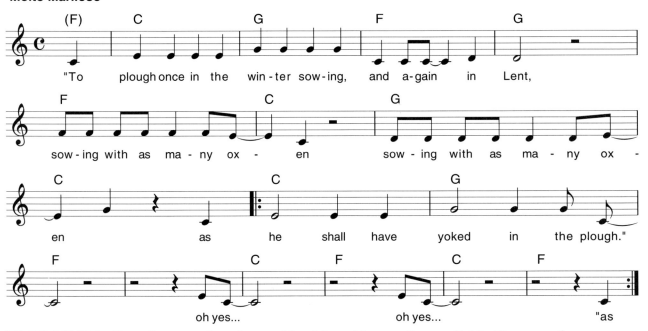

PROF. JONES: But of course there is considerable evidence of open-field villages as far
back as the tenth century. Professor Moorhead:

Poco Glitteroso

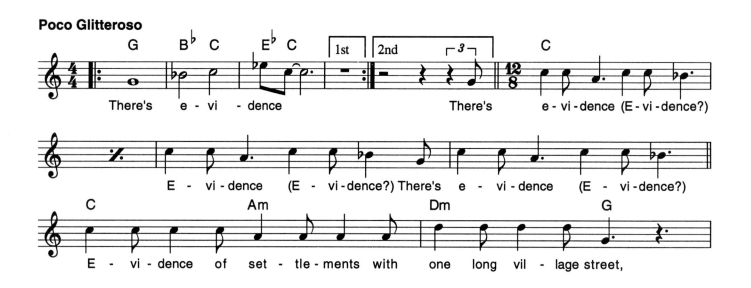

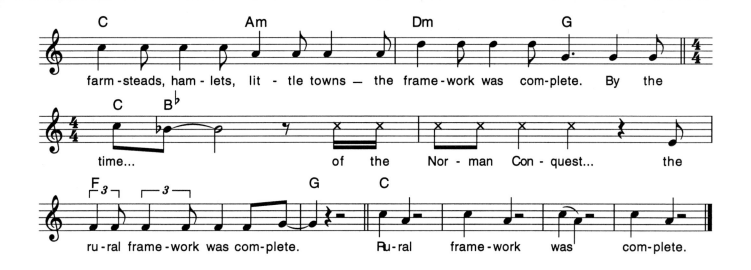

farm-steads, ham-lets, lit-tle towns — the frame-work was com-plete. By the

time... of the Nor-man Con-quest... the

ru-ral frame-work was com-plete. Ru-ral frame-work was com-plete.

PROF. JONES: This is not to say of course that the system was as sophisticated as it later came to be. I asked the Professor of Mediaeval Studies at Cambridge why this was.
PROF. HEGERMANN: Well it may not have been a statutory obligation, but I mean, a guy who was a freeman was obliged in the mediaeval system to...
PROF. JONES: To do boonwork?
PROF. HEGERMANN: That's right. There's an example from the village rolls in 1313.
PROF. JONES: And I believe you're going to do it for us.
PROF. HEGERMANN: That's right, yes...

Sempre Heyjudioso

(Oh) It's writ-ten in the vil-lage rolls that "if one

plough-team wants an ox - - en and that ox - en is

lent, then the vil - leins and the plough-man have

got to have the lord's con-sent." Then the

vil - leins and the plough-man got to have the lord's con-sent."

NEXT WEEK: The Background to History Part V: Professor K.L. Hislop, "Gay Clubs in Thirteenth Century Scotland"

AND NOW MR TERRY GILLIAM
WILL SING FOR YOU...

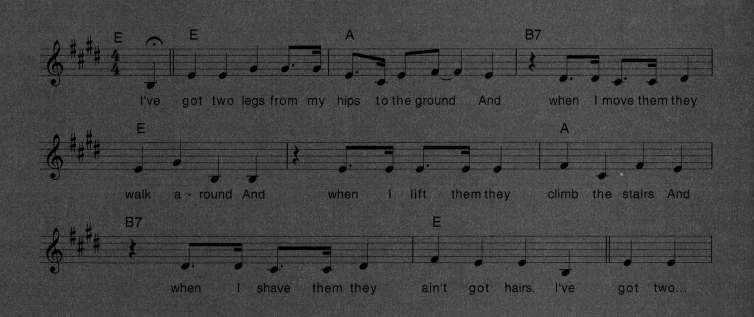

I've got two legs from my hips to the ground And when I move them they

walk a - round And when I lift them they climb the stairs And

when I shave them they ain't got hairs. I've got two...

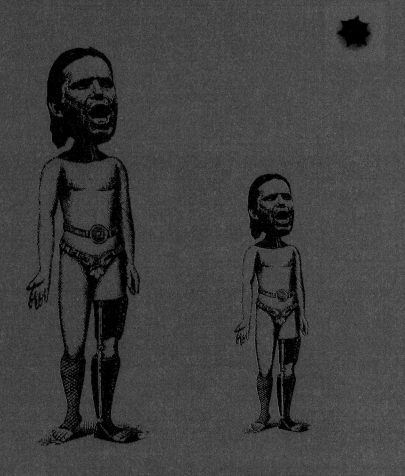

TODAY

Today I can hear the robin sing.

Today the thrush is on the wing.

Today who knows what life will bring? Today!

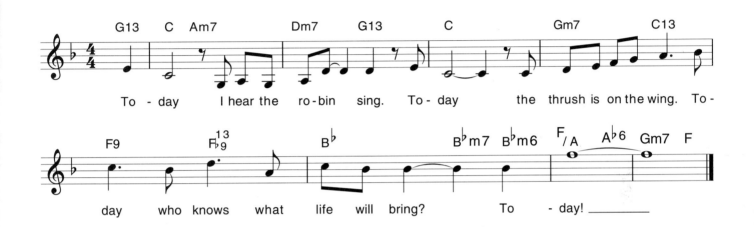

To - day   I hear the   ro-bin   sing.   To - day   the   thrush is on the wing.   To -

day   who knows   what   life   will   bring?   To   - day! _____

I'm so worried !

I'm so worried about what's happening today
In the Middle East, you know
And I'm so worried about the baggage retrieval
System they've got at Heathrow

I'm so worried about the fashions today
I don't think they're good for your feet
And I'm so worried about the shows on TV
That sometimes they want to repeat

I'm so worried about what's happening today, you know
And I'm worried about the baggage retrieval
System they've got at Heathrow

I'm so worried about my hair falling out
And the state of the world today
And I'm so worried about being so full of doubt
About everything anyway

I'm so worried about modern technology
I'm so worried about all the things that they dump in the sea
I'm so worried about it, worried about it
Worried, worried, worried...

I'm so worried about everything that can go wrong
I'm so worried about whether people like this song
I'm so worried about this very next verse
It isn't the best that I've got
And I'm so worried about whether I should go on
Or whether I shouldn't just stop

I'm worried about whether I ought to have stopped
And I'm worried because it's the sort of thing I ought to know
And I'm so worried about the baggage retrieval
System they've got at Heathrow

I'm so worried about whether I should have stopped then
I'm so worried that I'm driving everyone round the bend
I'm worried about the baggage retrieval
System they've got at Heathrow

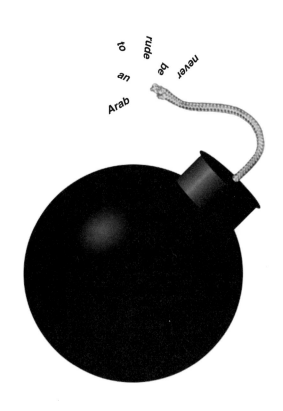

never be rude to an Arab

Fin-land, Fin-land, Fin-land, The coun-try where I want to
be, Po-ny trek-king or cam-ping Or just watch-ing T V
Fin-land, Fin-land, Fin-land, It's the coun-try for
me. You're so near to Rus-sia, So far from Ja-
pan Quite a long way from Cai-ro, Lots of miles from Viet-nam.

Finland, Finland, Finland
The country where I want to be
Eating breakfast or dinner
Or snack lunch in the hall
Finland, Finland, Finland
Finland has it all

You're so sadly neglected
And often ignored
A poor second to Belgium
When going abroad

Finland, Finland, Finland
The country where I quite want to be
Your mountains so lofty
Your treetops so tall
Finland, Finland, Finland
Finland has it all

Finland has it all...

All Things Dull & Ugly

All things dull and ugly
All creatures short and squat
All things rude and nasty
The Lord God made the lot

Each little snake that poisons
Each little wasp that stings
He made their brutish venom
He made their horrid wings

All things sick and cancerous
All evil great and small
All things foul and dangerous
The Lord God made them all

Each nasty little hornet
Each beastly little squid
Who made the spikey urchin?
Who made the sharks? He did.

All things scabbed and ulcerous
All pox both great and small
Putrid, foul and gangrenous
The Lord God made them all

AMEN

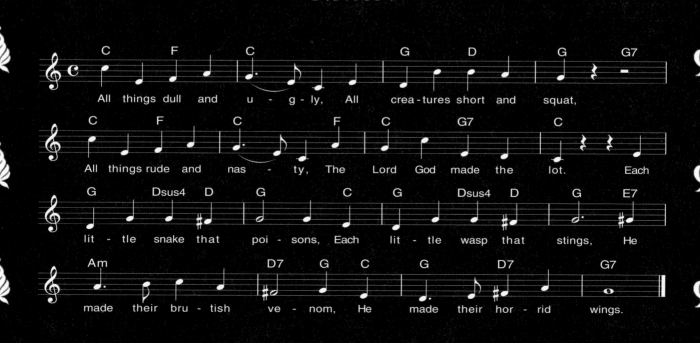

Claude Achille Debussy, died 1918. Christophe Willibald Gluck, died 1787. Carl Maria von Weber, not at all well 1825, died 1826. Giacomo Meyerbeer, still alive 1863, not still alive 1864. Modest Mussorgski, 1880 going to parties, no fun any more 1881. Johann Nepomuk Hummel, ch

Handel and Haydn and Rachmaninov
Enjoyed a nice drink with their meal
But nowadays no-one will serve them
And their gravy is left to congeal

Verdi and Wagner delighted the crowds
With their highly original sound
The pianos they played are still working
But they're both six feet underground

They're decomposing composers
There's less of them every year
You can say what you like to Debussy
But there's not much of him left to hear

decomposing

Afterword

by a prominent health specialist

Many people, after reading a book like this, may well prepare a salad or a *timbale des fruits* without washing their hands. This can lead to itching, discomfort and bottom problems.

It is *imperative* after reading explicitly musical material to wash, scrub, scour, or better still, sand-blast your hands before doing anything else. In fact, to be totally safe, we suggest you cut them off and put them somewhere well away from dirt. This does not mean you can make a salad with the stumps. In fact, if you want to avoid serious illness, don't make salad at all, or read books, or better still, be alive. I've been dead for over a year now and can honestly say I've never felt better.

Yours sincerely,

Brigadier N.Q.T.F. Sixpence (Mrs)

SPECIALLY SELECTED BY

SIGNOR CARUSO.

FOR SONGS THAT ARTISTS SING

Inflammation of the foreskin reminds me of your smile
I've had ballanital chancroids for quite a little while
I gave my heart to NSU that lovely night in June
I ache for you, my darling, and I hope you get well soon

A MEDICAL LOVE

§

SONG

WITH PIANO ACCOMPANIMENT, AD LIB.

WORDS BY

MR ERIC IDLE & DR GRAHAM CHAPMAN

~~~~~~

MUSIC BY

MR ERIC IDLE & PROF. JOHN DU PREZ

∞

ALSO PUBLISHED AS A VOCAL DUET IN KEYS E# & G

My clapped-out genitalia is not so bad for me
As the complete and utter failure every time I try to pee
My doctor says my buboes are the worst he's ever seen
My scrotum's painted orange and my balls are turning green

My heart is very tender though my parts are awful raw
You might have been infected but you never were a bore
I'm dying of your love, my love, I'm your spirochaetal clown
I've left my body to science but I'm afraid they've turned it down

§

COPYRIGHT MCMLXXX
BY THE KGB

KAY-GEE-BEE MUSIC LTD
& OCEAN MUSIC LTD

68a Delancey Street, London N.W.1

New York. Paris. Clapham Junction.

For surgical sports of all kinds

I like traffic lights,
I like traffic lights,
I like traffic lights,
No matter where they've been.

I like traffic lights,
I like traffic lights,
I like traffic lights,
I like traffic lights,
I like traffic lights,

But only when they're **green.** ■

He likes traffic lights,
He likes traffic lights,
He likes traffic lights,
No matter where they've been.

He likes traffic lights,
He likes traffic lights,
He likes traffic lights,
But only when they're green.

I like traffic lights,
I like traffic lights,
I like traffic lights,
That is what I said.

I like traffic lights,
I like traffic lights,
I like traffic lights,

But not when they are **red.** ■

He likes traffic lights,
He likes traffic lights,
That is what he said.

He likes traffic lights,
He likes traffic lights,
He likes traffic lights,
He likes traffic lights,
He likes traffic lights,
But not when they are red.

I like traffic lights,
I like traffic lights,
I like traffic lights,

Although my name's not **Bamber.** ■

I like traffic lights,
I like traffic lights,
I like traffic lights,
I...Oh God!

G

I like traf - fic lights, I like traf - fic lights, I like traf - fic lights, No
I like traf - fic lights, I like traf - fic lights, I like traf - fic lights, But

1st D7 G | 2nd Am D7 G

mat - ter where they've been. on - ly when they're green.

Brian... the babe they called Brian
He grew... grew, grew and grew
Grew up to be
Grew up to be
A boy called Brian
A boy called Brian

He had arms and legs and hands and feet
This boy whose name was Brian
And he grew... grew, grew and grew
Grew up to be
Yes he grew up to be
A teenager called Brian
A teenager called Brian

And his face became spotty
Yes his face became spotty
And his voice dropped down low
And things started to grow
On young Brian and show
He was certainly no
No girl named Brian
Not a girl named Brian

And he started to shave
And have one off the wrist
And want to see girls
And go out and get pissed
A man called Brian
This man called Brian
The man they called Brian
This man called Brian

Penis Song
not the Noël Coward Song

Good evening, ladies and gentlemen.
Here's a little number I tossed off recently
in the Caribbean.

Isn't it awfully nice to have a penis,
Isn't it frightfully good to have a dong?
It's swell to have a stiffy,
It's divine to own a dick,
From the tiniest little tadger,
To the world's biggest prick.

So three cheers for your Willy or John Thomas,
Hooray for your one-eyed trouser snake,
Your piece of pork, your wife's best friend,
Your Percy or your cock,
You can wrap it up in ribbons,
You can slip it in your sock,
But don't take it out in public,
Or they will stick you in the dock,
And you won't come back.

Middleword by E. F. God

When I created the world in those *amazingly* busy seven days, I remember it as being a tremendously exciting period. There was *so* much to do that I honestly had hardly any time to notice what I was creating. I know that sounds awful, but I think anyone who's created anything will realise that very often you become so tied up with whatever it is you're creating that you can't see the wood for the trees - and I was *creating* the wood and the trees!

I mean, some days were great. The first day of course we couldn't see a bloody thing. I mean, I actually had to invent light just so we could see what we were doing! Sounds crazy now, doesn't it! Once I'd got the hang of it and done the basics there were some very exciting moments, though. The firmament, which I did on the second day, was great because, to be quite honest, I had no idea what a firmament really was, I just had to have something to divide the waters from the waters, and it turned out to be just right for that purpose. I also liked the tree yielding fruit. I don't know, it just had a nice ring to it. I suppose, now, with the benefit of hindsight, perhaps I should have just stuck to the tree and forgotten the fruit, but I liked the fruit and I didn't know Adam and Eve would make such a bollocks of it (excuse my French). I've been quite criticised over the years for letting them loose in the Garden of Eden, but I gave them Free Will and they decided that rather than write poetry or sing to each other or invent a board game they'd go and talk to snakes. All right, I accept that there was an inherent risk but honestly, if you could have the choice to do anything you wanted in the loveliest garden ever made, with rivers and trees yielding fruit all over the place, would you seek out the nearest snake and ask how you could best get a rise out of the park-keeper? The next thing is that poor old Muggins is being blamed for everything from the Black Death to setting fire to Windsor Castle. There is no evidence in any of my utterances that I tampered with the wiring in the Long Gallery, just below the little French satinwood side-table where the Queen keeps the telephone directories, and if you can find the phrase "And then God created buboes", then all right, I decimated Europe, personally, in the fourteenth century. (I mean, I *created* Europe in the first place, why would I want to decimate it?) Sorry to go on but there is a downside to being Creator (my capitals).

Now various people have written to me and asked why I didn't create music and if I *had* created it would I have created reggae or funk or ska or something classical. Well, without getting too heavy I have to remind you that I created Man (and, call me a sexist pig, but some days I wish I'd left it there) and left him to come up with whatever he wanted. Well, we all know now that the silly sod chose sin, and that's water under the bridge, but I have to say that there are some things that he thought up which have given me a little quiet pride, and music is one of them. Now, a lot of what I call Brown-nose music, you know, all that "How Great Thou Art, Wonderful God" etc., etc., doesn't do a thing for me, and if I hear another organ I might well reconsider about the buboes. What I like is a song which just goes straight to the heart of things. What could summon up the joy of creation more than "Isn't It Frightfully Nice to Have a Penis"? I mean, thank you, whoever wrote that. Thank you. I was at my lowest ebb when I created the penis. It was, quite frankly, a rush job and I thought it looked a bit daft. So it's jolly good to hear someone thanking me for it. "I've Got Two Legs", there's another. It's all very well producing Organ Sonatas and Oratorios, but no one ever stops to consider that without two legs you can't reach the bloody pedals! (Excuse my French.) It is for all these reasons that I believe the Monty Python songs will live long after Mozart and Beethoven and Crispian St Peters have been forgotten. I can truly say that these songs are recommended by God.

ALWAYS LOOK ON THE BRIGHT SIDE OF...

ALWAYS LOOK ON THE BRIGHT SIDE OF...

LIFE

SOME THINGS IN LIFE ARE BAD
THEY CAN REALLY MAKE YOU MAD
OTHER THINGS JUST MAKE YOU SWEAR AND CURSE
WHEN YOU'RE CHEWING ON LIFE'S GRISTLE
DON'T GRUMBLE, GIVE A WHISTLE
AND THIS'LL HELP THINGS TURN OUT FOR THE BEST...

AND... ALWAYS LOOK ON THE BRIGHT SIDE OF LIFE...
ALWAYS LOOK ON THE LIGHT SIDE OF LIFE...

IF LIFE SEEMS JOLLY ROTTEN
THERE'S SOMETHING YOU'VE FORGOTTEN
AND THAT'S TO LAUGH AND SMILE AND DANCE AND SING
WHEN YOU'RE FEELING IN THE DUMPS
DON'T BE SILLY CHUMPS
JUST PURSE YOUR LIPS AND WHISTLE, THAT'S THE THING

AND... ALWAYS LOOK ON THE BRIGHT SIDE OF LIFE...
COME ON, ALWAYS LOOK ON THE BRIGHT SIDE OF LIFE...

FOR LIFE IS QUITE ABSURD
AND DEATH'S THE FINAL WORD
YOU MUST ALWAYS FACE THE CURTAIN WITH A BOW
FORGET ABOUT YOUR SIN, GIVE THE AUDIENCE A GRIN
ENJOY IT, IT'S YOUR LAST CHANCE ANYHOW
SO ALWAYS LOOK ON THE BRIGHT SIDE OF DEATH
JUST BEFORE YOU DRAW YOUR TERMINAL BREATH
LIFE'S A PIECE OF SHIT
WHEN YOU LOOK AT IT
LIFE'S A LAUGH AND DEATH'S A JOKE, IT'S TRUE
YOU'LL SEE IT'S ALL A SHOW
KEEP 'EM LAUGHING AS YOU GO
JUST REMEMBER THAT THE LAST LAUGH IS ON YOU

AND... ALWAYS LOOK ON THE BRIGHT SIDE OF LIFE...
ALWAYS LOOK ON THE RIGHT SIDE OF LIFE...
COME ON GUYS, CHEER UP
ALWAYS LOOK ON THE BRIGHT SIDE OF LIFE...
ALWAYS LOOK ON THE BRIGHT SIDE OF LIFE...

WORSE THINGS HAPPEN AT SEA, YOU KNOW
ALWAYS LOOK ON THE BRIGHT SIDE OF LIFE...
I MEAN, WHAT HAVE YOU GOT TO LOSE?
YOU KNOW, YOU COME FROM NOTHING
YOU'RE GOING BACK TO NOTHING
WHAT HAVE YOU LOST? NOTHING!

ALWAYS LOOK ON THE RIGHT SIDE OF LIFE...

Christmas in Heaven

Slow   Bb   Cm7   F7

It's Christ-mas in Hea-ven, All the child-ren sing, It's Christ-mas in Hea-ven, Hark

Bb   Eb/F   Bb

hark those church bells ring It's Christ-mas in Hea-ven, the

Cm7   F7

snow falls from the sky... But it's nice and warm and e-very-one Looks

Eb   Bb **(Double Speed)**   Bb

smart and wears a tie. It's Christ-mas in Hea-ven, There's

Cm7   F7

great films on T V   *The Sound of Mu - sic* twice an hour And

Bb   Eb/F   Bb

Jaws I II and III There's gifts for all the fam - i - ly, There's

Cm7   F7

toi - let - ries and trains There's So-ny Walk-man head-phone sets And the

Bb   **CHORUS** Bb

la - test vi - de - o games! It's Christ-mas It's Christ-mas in Hea-ven,

F7   Bb

Hip hip hip hip hip hoo - ray, E-very sin-gle day, It's Christ-mas Day.

ACCOUNTANCY SHANTY: It's fun to charter an accountant and sail the wide accountan - cy, to find, explore the funds offshore and skirt the shoals of bankruptcy, It can be manly in insurance; we'll up your premium semi - annually, it's all tax - deductible, we're fairly incorruptible, we're sailing on the wide accountan - cy!

Accountant Sea Shanty

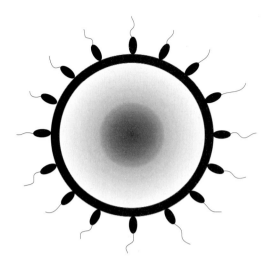

EVERY
Sperm
IS SACRED

There are Jews in the world,
There are Buddhists,
There are Hindus and Mormons and then,
There are those that follow Mohammed,
But I've never been one of them...
I'm a Roman Catholic,
And have been since before I was born,
And the one thing they say about Catholics,
Is they'll take you as soon as you're warm...
You don't have to be a six-footer,
You don't have to have a great brain,
You don't have to have any clothes on
You're a Catholic the moment Dad came...
Because...

Every sperm is sacred,
Every sperm is great,
If a sperm is wasted,
God gets quite irate.

Let the heathen spill theirs,
On the dusty ground,
God shall make them pay for
Each sperm that can't be found.

Every sperm is wanted,
Every sperm is good,
Every sperm is needed
In your neighbourhood.

Hindu, Taoist, Mormon,
Spill theirs just anywhere,
But God loves those who treat their
Semen with more care.

Every sperm is sacred,
Every sperm is great,
If a sperm is wasted,
God gets quite irate.

Every sperm is sacred,
Every sperm is good,
Every sperm is needed
In your neighbourhood.

Every sperm is useful,
Every sperm is fine,
God needs everybody's,
Mine!
And mine!
And mine!

Let the pagan spill theirs,
O'er mountain, hill and plain,
God shall strike them down for
Each sperm that's spilt in vain.

Every sperm is sacred,
Every sperm is good,
Every sperm is needed
In your neighbourhood.

Every sperm is sacred,
Every sperm is great,
If a sperm is wasted,
God gets quite irate.

Jelusarem.

And did those feet in an-cient time wark u-pon Eng-rand's moun-tains gleen? And was the ho—ry Ramb of God on Eng-rand's prea-sant pas-tules seen? And did the Coun-te-nance Di-vine shine folth u-pon our croud-ed hirrs? And was Je-lu-sa-rem buir-ded here a-mong these dark Sa-ta-nic mirrs?

Bling me my bow of bulning gord!
Bling me my allows of desile!
Bling me my speal! O crouds unford!
Bling me my chaliot of file!
I sharr not cease flom Mentar Fight
Nol sharr my Swold sreep in my hand,
Tirr we have buirt Jelusarem
In Engrand's gleen and preasant Rand.

Why are we here, what's life all about? Is God really real, or is there some doubt? Well, tonight we're going to sort it all out, for tonight it's the Meaning of Life. What's the point of all this hoax? Is it the chicken and the egg time, are we just yolks? Or perhaps we're just one of God's little jokes, well, *ça c'est* the Meaning of Life. Is life just a game where we make up the rules, while we're searching for something to say, or are we just simply spiralling coils of self-replicating DNA? In this life, what is our fate? Is there Heaven and Hell? Do we reincarnate? Is mankind evolving or is it too late? Well, tonight here's the Meaning of Life. For millions this life is a sad vale of tears, sitting round with *rien,* nothing to say, while the scientists say we're just simply spiralling coils of self-replicating DNA. So just why, why are we here? And just what, what, what, what do we fear? Well *ce soir,* for a change, it will all be made clear, for this is the Meaning of Life – *c'est le sens de la vie* – this is the Meaning of Life.

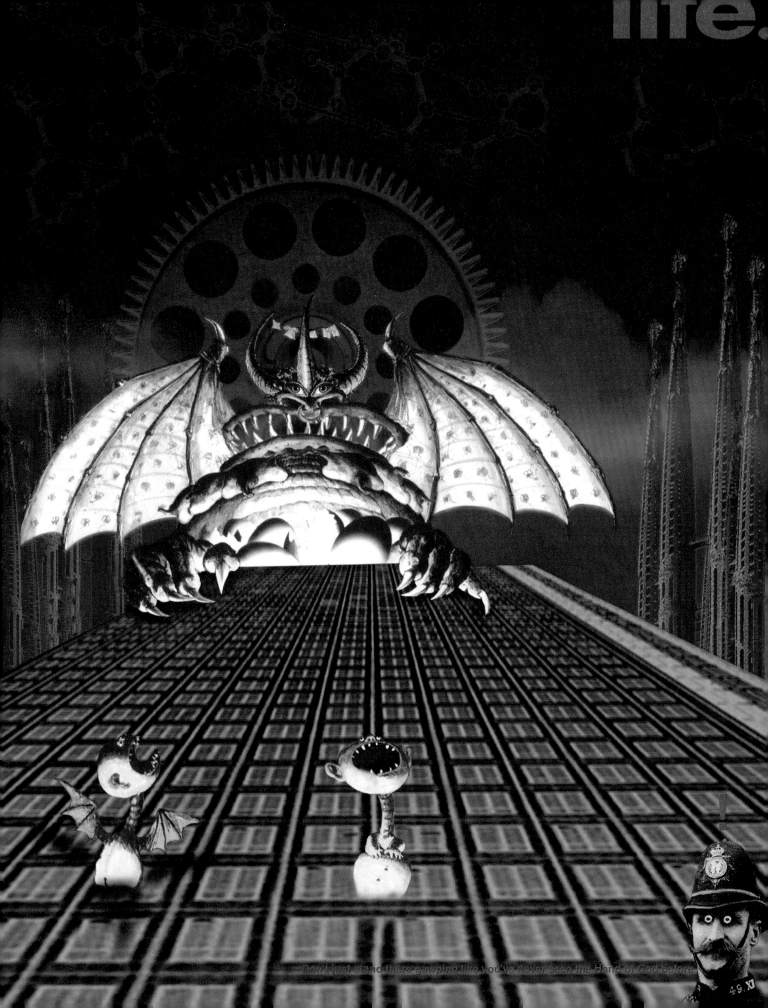

Don't just stand there gawping like you've never seen the Hand of God before.

49.XI

SONG

Whenever life gets you down, Mrs Brown, and things seem hard or tough, and
people are stupid, obnoxious or daft, and you feel that you've had quite enough...

Our Galaxy itself contains 100 billion stars

It's 100,000 light years side to side,

It bulges in the middle, 16,000 light years thick

But out by us it's just 3,000 light years wide

We're 30,000 light years from galactic central point,

We go round every 200 million years

And our Galaxy is only one of millions of billions

In this amazing and expanding Universe.

The Universe itself keeps on expanding and expanding

In all of the directions it can whizz

As fast as it can go, at the speed of light you know,

12 million miles a minute, and that's the fastest speed there is.

So remember when you're feeling very small and insecure

How amazingly unlikely is your birth

And pray that there's intelligent life somewhere up in space

Because there's bugger all down here on Earth.

YOU ARE HERE

TITLE	MUSIC	WORDS	PUBLISHER	SOURCE
Accountancy Shanty	E. Idle, J. Du Prez	E. Idle, J. Du Prez	© 1983 Kay-Gee-Bee Music Ltd	Meaning of Life
All Things Dull and Ugly	Trad., arr. J. Du Prez	Eric Idle	© 1980 Kay-Gee-Bee Music Ltd	Contractual Obligation
Always Look on the Bright Side	Eric Idle	Eric Idle	© 1979 Kay-Gee-Bee Music Ltd	Life of Brian
Anything Goes	Terry Jones	Terry Jones	© 1974 Kay-Gee-Bee Music Ltd	Flying Circus
Background to History	Neil Innes	Neil Innes	© 1974 EMI United Partnership, London WC2H OEA	Matching Tie
Bing Tiddle Tiddle Bong	Fred Tomlinson	Graham Chapman	© 1970 Kay-Gee-Bee Music Ltd	Flying Circus
Brave Sir Robin	Neil Innes	Eric Idle	© 1975 EMI United Partnership/ Kay-Gee-Bee Music Ltd, London WC2H OEA	Holy Grail
Brian	D. Howman, A. Jacquemin	Michael Palin	© 1979 Kay-Gee-Bee Music Ltd	Life of Brian
Bruces' Philosophers Song	Eric Idle	Eric Idle	© 1973 Kay-Gee-Bee Music Ltd	Matching Tie
Christmas in Heaven	Eric Idle	Terry Jones	© 1983 Kay-Gee-Bee Music Ltd	Meaning of Life
Decomposing Composers	Michael Palin	Michael Palin	© 1980 Kay-Gee-Bee Music Ltd	Contractual Obligation
Dennis Moore	What music?	G. Chapman, J. Cleese	Lyrics © 1972 Kay-Gee-Bee Music Ltd	Flying Circus/ Previous Record
Do What John?	Eric Idle	Eric Idle	© 1980 Kay-Gee-Bee Music Ltd	Contractual Obligation
Eric the Half a Bee	Eric Idle	E. Idle, J. Cleese	© 1972 Kay-Gee-Bee Music Ltd	Previous Record
Every Sperm is Sacred	D. Howman, A. Jacquemin	M. Palin, T. Jones	© 1983 Kay-Gee-Bee Music Ltd	Meaning of Life
Ferret Song	Bob Leaper	J. Cleese, G. Chapman	© 1967 Noel Gay Music Co. Ltd	At Last the 1948 Show
Finland	Michael Palin	Michael Palin	© 1980 Kay-Gee-Bee Music Ltd	Contractual Obligation
Galaxy Song	E. Idle, J. Du Prez	Eric Idle	© 1983 Kay-Gee-Bee Music Ltd	Meaning of Life
Henry Kissinger	Eric Idle	Eric Idle	© 1980 Kay-Gee-Bee Music Ltd	Contractual Obligation
Here Comes Another One	Terry Jones	Terry Jones	© 1980 Kay-Gee-Bee Music Ltd	Contractual Obligation
Holzfällerliederhosen	M. Palin, T. Jones, F. Tomlinson	M. Palin, T. Jones	© 1972 Kay-Gee-Bee Music Ltd	Fliegender Zirkus
I Bet You They Won't Play...	Eric Idle	Eric Idle	© 1980 Kay-Gee-Bee Music Ltd	Contractual Obligation
I Like Chinese	Eric Idle	Eric Idle	© 1980 Kay-Gee-Bee Music Ltd	Contractual Obligation
I Like Traffic Lights	Terry Jones	Terry Jones	© 1980 Kay-Gee-Bee Music Ltd	Contractual Obligation
I'm So Worried	Terry Jones	Terry Jones	© 1980 Kay-Gee-Bee Music Ltd	Contractual Obligation
I've Got Two Legs	Terry Gilliam	Terry Gilliam	© 1981 Kay-Gee-Bee Music Ltd	Live at Drury Lane
Jelusarem	Sir Hubert Parry	W. Blake, G. Chapman	© 1972 Kay-Gee-Bee Music Ltd	
Knights of the Round Table	Neil Innes	G. Chapman, J. Cleese	© 1975 EMI United Partnership/ Kay-Gee-Bee Music Ltd, London WC2H OEA	Holy Grail
Lumberjack Song	M. Palin, T. Jones, F. Tomlinson	M. Palin, T. Jones	© 1969 Kay-Gee-Bee Music Ltd	Flying Circus
Meaning of Life	E. Idle, J. Du Prez	Eric Idle	© 1983 Kay-Gee-Bee Music Ltd	Meaning of Life
Medical Love Song	E. Idle, J. Du Prez	E. Idle, G. Chapman	© 1980 Kay-Gee-Bee Music Ltd/ Ocean Music Ltd	Contractual Obligation
Money Song	John Gould	E. Idle, J. Gould	© 1972 Kay-Gee-Bee Music Ltd	Previous Record
Muddy Knees	Terry Jones	Terry Jones	© 1980 Kay-Gee-Bee Music Ltd	Contractual Obligation
Never be Rude to an Arab	Terry Jones	Terry Jones	© 1980 Kay-Gee-Bee Music Ltd	Contractual Obligation
O Lord Please Don't Burn Us	John Du Prez	G. Chapman, J. Cleese	© 1983 Kay-Gee-Bee Music Ltd	Meaning of Life
Oliver Cromwell	Chopin, arr. J. Du Prez	John Cleese	© 1980 Kay-Gee-Bee Music Ltd	Monty Python Sings
Penis Song (Not Noë! Coward)	Eric Idle	Eric Idle	© 1983 Kay-Gee-Bee Music Ltd	Meaning of Life
Proust Song	Fred Tomlinson	Fred Tomlinson	© 1972 Kay-Gee-Bee Music Ltd	Previous Record
Rhubarb Tart Song	John Cleese	John Cleese	© 1967 Noel Gay Music Co. Ltd	At Last the 1948 Show
Sit on my Face	Harry Parr Davies	Eric Idle	© 1934 Francis Day & Hunter, London WC2H OEA. New lyrics © 1980 Francis Day & Hunter, London WC2H OEA	Contractual Obligation
Spam Song	M. Palin, T. Jones, F. Tomlinson	M. Palin, T. Jones	© 1970 Kay-Gee-Bee Music Ltd	Flying Circus
Today	Bill McGuffie	Bill McGuffie	© 1970 Kay-Gee-Bee Music Ltd	Flying Circus
Ya Di Bucketty	Terry Jones	T. Jones, J. Cleese	© 1972 Kay-Gee-Bee Music Ltd	Previous Record
Yangtse Song	M. Palin, T. Jones, N. Innes	M. Palin, T. Jones	© 1972 Kay-Gee-Bee Music Ltd	Previous Record

This book was originally published in Great Britain in 1994 by Methuen London, an imprint of Reed Consumer Books Ltd.

Designed by Gary Marsh at Gone Loco
with assistance from John Hurst and Mary O'Donovan
Music edited by John Du Prez
Co-ordinated by Roger Saunders

ISBN 0-06-095116-8

95 96 97 98 99 RRD 10 9 8 7 6 5 4 3 2 1

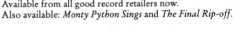